GYPSY QUEEN

by Rob Ward

Can two men raised to fight ever learn to love?

Published by Playdead Press 2022

© Rob Ward 2022

Rob Ward has asserted his rights under the Copyright, Design and Patents Act, 1988, to be identified as the author of this work.

A CIP catalogue record for this book is available from the British Library.

ISBN 978-1-915533-09-8

Caution

All rights whatsoever in this play are strictly reserved and application for performance should be sought through the author before rehearsals begin. No performance may be given unless a license has been obtained.

This book is sold subject to the condition that it shall not by way of trade or otherwise, be lent, resold, hired out, or otherwise circulated without the publisher's prior consent in any form of binding or cover other than that in which it is published and without a similar condition including this condition being imposed on the subsequent purchaser.

Playdead Press
www.playdeadpress.com

Gypsy Queen was first performed on 16th September 2016 at the John Thaw Studio of the Martin Harris Centre, part of the University of Manchester. It was a Hive North (formerly Hope Theatre Company) Production. The company was as follows:

'GORGEOUS' GEORGE O'CONNELL | **Rob Ward**

DANE 'THE PAIN' SAMSON | **Ryan Clayton**

Writer and Producer | **Rob Ward**
Director and Dramaturg | **Adam Zane**
Set Design | **Meriel Pym**
Sound Design and Stage Manager | **Owen Rafferty**

The production was revised for a UK tour in 2019, launching on 27th January at Moss Side Fire Station Boxing Club. It was an Emmerson & Ward Production.

'GORGEOUS' GEORGE O'CONNELL | **Rob Ward**

DANE 'THE PAIN' SAMSON | **John Askew**

Director | **Chris Lawson**
Producer | **Max Emmerson and Rob Ward**
Set Design | **Meriel Pym**
Sound Design | **Owen Rafferty**
Stage Manager | **Sophie Tetlow**

Rob Ward | Writer and Performer

Rob Ward is a writer, performer and co-director of Emmerson & Ward Productions. His 2013 play *Away From Home* (co-written with Martin Jameson) toured nationally and internationally between 2013 and 2015, picking up the Manchester Theatre Awards for Best New Play and Best Fringe Performance. His 2016 play *Gypsy Queen* has also toured nationally and internationally since it premiered on the West End (Arts Theatre) and has gained critical acclaim. In 2017 Rob was named one of the British Council's Emerging Artists. Both of these plays dealt with the subject of homophobia and LGBT+ visibility in sport as well as other takes on modern queer identity. Rob has since written *Conversations* (Digital production commissioned by Curve in 2021) and *Love It If We Beat Them* (commissioned by Live Theatre) is currently in development.

John Askew | Performer

John trained at ArtsEd and his credits include:
Theatre: *Road* (Oldham Coliseum), *Rita, Sue and Bob Too* (Out of Joint/UK Tour), *And Did Those Feet* (Bolton Octagon), *Gypsy Queen* (UK and International Tour), *Harvest* (New Perspectives/UK Tour), *Wuthering Heights, Ladies in Lavender, Rope, Hay Fever* (Theatre Royal Windsor), *The Revengers Tragedy* (Nottingham Playhouse), Darkness Darkness (New Perspectives/Nottingham Playhouse), *Romeo & Juliet* (Buxton Opera House), *An Ideal Husband* (New Street, Jersey), *The Importance Of Being Earnest* (St. James Theatre, West End), *The Glasshouse* (Tristan Bates Theatre, West End), *Travesti* (Pleasance), *Christopher And His Kind* (UK Tour), *Sing Sing Sing* (UK Tour), *The Tempest* (UK Tour), *Don Juan* (UK Tour) and *40 Years On* (York Theatre Royal).

Television: *The English Game* (Netflix), *Flack* (Amazon Prime), *The Rook* (Lionsgate/Starz), *Doctors* (BBC), *Shameless* (Channel 4) and *Spooks: Code 9* (BBC). Radio: *The Legend of Robin Hood* (Augustine), *Killer By Nature*, *Unheard* (Audible) and *Dark Shadows* (Big Finish).

Ryan Clayton | Performer

Ryan is a Manchester born actor who trained at ALRA between 2012 and 2015. A great lover of all things Manchester City.

Credits include: *Waterloo Road*, *Coronation Street*, *Exile*, *Box Of Tricks*, *Gypsy Queen*.

Chris Lawson | Director

Chris is Oldham Coliseum Theatre's Artistic Director.

His previous shows at the Coliseum include: Beryl, *Aladdin*, *Four Minutes Twelve Seconds*, *Jack and the Beanstalk*, *Visitors*, *A Skull in Connemara*, *A Taste of Honey*, *The Kitchen Sink*, *Up N Under*, *Hard Times* and *Jumpers for Goalposts*. He also assisted on the Coliseum's productions of *Pygmalion* and *The Pitmen Painters*.

Chris' most recent production outside of Oldham was the international tour of *Gypsy Queen* by Rob Ward (Emmerson and Ward Productions). In December 2018 he directed his first pantomime, *Robin Hood and the Babes in the Wood* at CAST, Doncaster. As a theatre director, Chris has worked across the country following his original training at Bretton Hall, The University of Leeds, and later at RADA and Birkbeck, where he completed his Master's in Text and Performance.

CHARACTERS

This is a play designed for two actors to perform. The main characters are:

'Gorgeous' George O'Connell | Mid 20s. Lean and toned with a shaved head and beard. A bare knuckle fighter from an Irish traveller family, raised in the north of England. Northern.

Dane 'The Pain' Samson | Early 20s. Muscular build, tough looking. A professional boxer and the son of Vic. Northern.

Other characters, to be split between the two performers, include:

Vic Samson | Early 50s. Former professional boxer. Stiff physicality. Father and trainer to Dane. Northern.

Rose O'Connell | Mid 40s. Traveller and mother to George. A gentle tone but a sharp tongue if crossed. Irish.

Josh Benson | Early 20s. A fun and feisty little twink. Dane's fuck buddy. Scouse.

Connor O'Connell | Mid 20s. Irish traveller and cousin to George. Feckless. Irish.

Ivy Collins | 16. Lined up as George's potential wife. Traveller family. Scouse.

Andy Harris | 60s. Vic's second in command at the gym. Hoarse and gruff. Northern.

Scene One

The stage is split between two boxers, two worlds.

'Gorgeous' George O'Connell is preparing for a bare knuckle scrap in a pub car park. Dane 'The Pain' Samson readies himself for a professional bout.

GEORGE: It's all a show. A game. Whether it's arena lights, Olympic lights or, in my case, streetlights. This. A country lane near a car park. The outside of the outskirts of nowhere. Lovely evening for a scrap.

DANE: Arena filling up. Lights shine bright. I'm in the corner. The plan is hatched. This may be the undercard but I'm the main event. The Samson name commands the ring. Ding ding!

GEORGE: Tonight's challenge to this Gypsy King comes from the Carroll clan. Mick, their number one man, lumbers up, foams at the mouth, growls, a guard dog.

I flick the switch.

I'm Gorgeous George.

BOTH: Bang!

DANE: I stand centre of the ring, wind in my sails, fire in my belly. Shaun Wright, a journeyman from Flannigans' gym, prowls with little purpose.

>   Double jab, a right for fun. Step back and
>   repeat. Stay on the beat.

GEORGE: From the off old Mick charges in. Slides on the dirt track. Foot slips, wet grass. And down he falls into bed with a pile of dog dirt on a vine green throne.

>   Cracking start.

DANE: Dance back. Lungs full, I'm *Raging Bull*. The party's started, but there's a killjoy in the corner.

>   Vic, my dad and trainer. Former
>   middleweight champion of the world. Once
>   upon a time these people came for him. He
>   was their champion, he was their light. But
>   it soon went dark and he's lost without the
>   fight.

>   He's a bulldog chewing a hornet's nest.

VIC: Prancing like a pony. It's not dressage son. Where's that bang? Killer instinct?

DANE: Killer instinct. That'll be etched on his fucking grave.

>   Then Andy, second in command, takes over.
>   Water to the face, always misses the mouth.

Andy squirts a bottle of water into Dane's face before taking a swig of it himself.

>   You can rely on Andy for a cliché or two.

ANDY: You've got to roll with the punches. Take each round as it comes. He's got a chin sticking out like Bruce Forsythe, lamp him one!

DANE: And with those wise words of wisdom...he steps out of the ring, trips on the rope *(we hear Andy moan as he trips)* and I'm out for the fifth.

GEORGE: Dive in, land a right, duck out, gone from sight.

I try to catch Mick's eye to see how long is left. It's not easy. Mick's got one eye shooting east and one eye shooting west. But then, if your father will fuck his sister, what do you expect?

DANE: I'm a puzzle he can't solve. A code he can't crack. Nothing more needs doing. I'm playing this just right.

But back to the corner and Vic's nowhere in sight. Andy can't meet my eye.

Where's he gone?

Andy mumbles something inaudible.

DANE: Andy, where is he?

ANDY: Said something about having to be somewhere.

DANE: That's more important than here?

ANDY: *(gesturing to the other corner)* Take it out on him. This should've been finished rounds ago. You're sending this lot *(indicates crowd)* to sleep.

DANE: What dad does that?

Andy turns away.

DANE: Andy? Andy!

(of Vic) What a bastard!

GEORGE: BANG! *(Throws an uppercut)* Uppercut takes off his head.

After the fall it's Gorgeous George standing tall.

DANE: And winner by unanimous decision Dane 'The Pain' Samson.

GEORGE: We're vultures. Vermin. It's not fighting, it's scrapping. With our faces in the dirt. But I'm the prize face so I must be dirtier than all.

Back to the arena.

DANE: I look out to the crowd. Occasional smiles polite applause. And I wanna go all Russell Crowe. Are you not entertained? That old man is finished, the future is right here.

GEORGE: Don't believe everything you see, it's just a song I sing.

DANE: I stand in lights but right now the wrong Samson's in the ring.

Scene Two

An old country pub with a packed crowd.

GEORGE: After the fight, the Ship Inn. It's an old-fashioned, shit-stinking sup house. There's cock rock on the jukebox and three-tooth Tina behind the bar. A hero's reception.

A chorus of travellers chanting 'Gorgeous George na na na, Gorgeous George na na na' is heard.

CONNOR: *(chanting)* Gorgeous George na na na! Gorgeous George na na na!

GEORGE: *(To audience)* My cousin, Connor O'Connell. As much an eejit as his name suggests but decent, loyal.

CONNOR: Grand job George.

GEORGE: I've something for you.

CONNOR: What?

GEORGE: The purse.

CONNOR: Don't be handing me no fucking purse now.

GEORGE: The money from the fight.

CONNOR: What you giving it me for?

GEORGE: Mille.

Beat.

CONNOR: You're not serious.

GEORGE: I am.

CONNOR: I can't have you doing that for my daughter.

GEORGE: She's an O'Connell, so that's that.

Connor grabs George and gives him a huge hug.

CONNOR: You're the best. Look at you. Not even a scratch on that face Gorgeous George. Listen, I've been thinking…

CONNOR: Bet that hurt.

GEORGE: I want you to train me.

GEORGE: You?

CONNOR: You can be like yer man McGuigan. Leading the next generation.

GEORGE: It's not for you Connor.

CONNOR: I think I'll decide what's for me.

GEORGE: No, the guy who sparks you clean out will decide that.

CONNOR: I'm not feeling the love here.

GEORGE: It's a stupid idea.

CONNOR: George. Come on now. I'm not joking. Family is family.

GEORGE: I'll think about it.

CONNOR: I should think so. You wanna start remembering who you are, now you're living in that nice little city flat.

GEORGE: *(teasing)* You might be able to afford one some day.

CONNOR: I mean it. I don't like you being out of sight.

GEORGE: Well as you miss me that much Connor, I'll do it. I'll train you.

CONNOR: You will?

GEORGE: I will.

CONNOR: That's the spirit! Time to pass the baton. Let me take the O'Connells down the home straight.

Connor smiles at George and goes to leave.

CONNOR: Same again?

Connor leaves. George turns to audience.

GEORGE: Don't mind if I do. Three more in fact. Tina keeps the ale flowing and the night kicks in.

But a lone wolf stands in the corner, nose broken twice beyond repair. Danced around the ring so fast in his prime, but now he moves with little ease.

Vic Samson.

Vic approaches.

VIC: Alright George.

GEORGE: Stumbled into the wrong part of town? Speak foe, not friend.

VIC: We're not in Middle Earth son. No need to talk like fucking Gandalf.

GEORGE: Credit to you. Balls the size of coconuts.

VIC: I believe congratulations are in order. Still undefeated.

GEORGE: Niceties very much appreciated. But I'm not sure that's why you're here.

VIC: I'm here to make you rich a man?

GEORGE: Someone said that to my dad once.

VIC: Well that someone were a dick head. He were a good scrapper your dad, but a weak boxer.

GEORGE: Come earn some proper cash they said. Stuck him in the ring with you. Fifty seconds was it?

VIC: Forty five.

GEORGE: I'd take you out in forty.

VIC: Come prove it then. Come train with me and every boxing fan in this country will sing your name.

GEORGE: Gonna take more than that. I'm king round here.

VIC: So this gonna be it for you? Scrapping in country lanes and getting pissed on her dodgy ale.

GEORGE: She's alright is Tina. Single too. I could put a word in for you. Must have been a while.

VIC: I do alright!

I mean it George. Don't waste your talent son. You're an animal. I like that. I can work with that.

A chorus of 'Gorgeous George na na na' is heard

GEORGE: My people await.

VIC: Immortality, George. Think about it.

Scene Three

Josh's bedroom. Dane and Josh have just had sex. Josh lies in ecstasy.

JOSH: Frig me sideways!

Dane starts getting changed.

JOSH: Where do you think you're going? I want round two.

DANE: I've got to go Josh.

JOSH: Aren't you gonna tell me about your fight?

DANE: What d'you wanna know?

JOSH: Well, did you win?

DANE: Yeah.

JOSH: Who was you fighting?

DANE: Just this bloke. Shaun Wright.

JOSH: Sounds hot.

DANE: He's a big fat fucker.

JOSH: Well what are you doing fighting a big fat fucker when you're fit as fuck?

DANE: We're the same weight.

JOSH: But with him it's all man boobs and blubber and you it's all muscle.

DANE: Something like that.

JOSH: Show us how you do it then, this boxing. Is it like this?

Josh enthusiastically jumps up and adopts a camp boxer's pose.

DANE: What are you doing?

JOSH: Or like this?

Josh changes his stance, still camper than Christmas.

DANE: What's that? You look like a velociraptor.

JOSH: Show me then!

Dane coaches Josh.

DANE: Legs apart. You should be used to that.

JOSH: Oi!

DANE: That there is your jab. And that is your hook.

JOSH: *(following instructions)* Jab, hook. Jab, hook. Jab, hook.

DANE: Butch up.

He digs Josh in the stomach.

JOSH: Oh, I can't take no more. The winner is Dane Samson.

DANE: Dane 'The Pain' Samson.

JOSH: You what?

DANE: We have nicknames.

JOSH: Like on Gladiators?

DANE: 'The Hitman', 'The Executioner'.

JOSH: And what was yours again?

DANE: The Pain.

Josh bursts out laughing.

JOSH: Give over.

DANE: It is.

JOSH: Pain in the arse more like.

Dane smiles wryly at Josh.

JOSH: So what would my nickname be?

DANE: Whatever you want it to be.

JOSH: Josh 'The Bottom' Benson.

(adopts commentator's voice) "And The Bottom is face down, peachy cheeks up in the air, ripe for plucking."

Come on; show us your knockout blow.

DANE: It wasn't a knockout.

JOSH: Well how did you win?

DANE: On points.

JOSH: There's points as well?

DANE: Yes.

JOSH: Friggin' hell it's complicated this boxing. Who gives out the points?

DANE: Judges.

JOSH: Like on *Strictly*?

DANE: No nothing like *Strictly*.

JOSH: *(impersonating Len Goodman)* Seven!

DANE: I need to go.

JOSH: So are you the champion now?

DANE: Not yet.

JOSH: Well you're my champion.

This makes Dane uncomfortable. Josh realises this.

JOSH: Oh, before I forget. My mum's doing one of her fancy meals.

DANE: Ok.

JOSH: Dauphinoise potatoes. She said I could invite me mystery fella.

DANE: Right.

JOSH: It's a couple of weeks off yet so have a think.

DANE: I'd better go.

JOSH: Can we spoon for five more minutes?

DANE: Maybe next time.

Scene Four

A travellers' campsite. George enters his mother Rose's caravan and gives her a kiss on the cheek.

ROSE: Will you shave that beard? You look like something that cocks its leg for a piss.

GEORGE: How are you ma?

ROSE: Still here.

GEORGE: And looking well for it.

ROSE: Did you see my ornamental butterflies?

GEORGE: The ones outside the van? I did, yeah.

ROSE: That big purple one, that's Betty. After your great nan. Betty the Butterfly. She'd have loved that. Aren't they beautiful? My own little zoo of butterflies.

GEORGE: I like what you've done to the van. You get Little Bill and Bobby Roy round again?

ROSE: Loves his Aunty Rose does Little Bill. He gave it a lick of paint. That Bobby Roy was too busy licking windows. He's awful gormless that boy. Stares so long he turns day to night.

So where have you been hiding yourself?

GEORGE: Been in training for the Carroll fight. You heard the good news?

George takes a seat next to Rose.

ROSE: I heard. I hope that's to be the end of it now George. I don't want to be sticking your eyeball back into its socket.

GEORGE: Don't be dramatic.

ROSE: Dramatic! I was there. Out here your father's eye was. Talk to me like that you little cunt!

GEORGE: Okay ma, okay.

ROSE: Will you have a brew?

GEORGE: Aye go on.

George spots a plate of Jammie Dodgers.

GEORGE: I'm definitely having one of those.

George grabs one, dips it in his brew and bites into it.

ROSE: Will you not say grace?

GEORGE: Are you serious?

ROSE: Perfectly.

GEORGE: It's a Jammie Dodger.

ROSE: George O'Connell, our lord died for our sins so you could sit there and stuff your face…

GEORGE: Right okay. For what we're about to receive may the lord make us truly thankful.

ROSE: Put something into it.

GEORGE:	*(with more sincerity)* For what we're about to receive may the lord make us truly thankful.
ROSE:	*(chuckling)* Course you don't need to say it for a Jammie Dodger. I was checking you remembered grace. There's been more sightings of Lord fucking Lucan than you at mass.
GEORGE:	I'll go with you Sunday.
ROSE:	Now then young man. What happened to this girl? Colette was it?
GEORGE:	Bernadette.
ROSE:	Bernadette! Lovely girl.
GEORGE:	I didn't like her ma.
ROSE:	You're going to be 27 years old soon. But rather than court a nice girl, you're out sewing your wild oats.
GEORGE:	I didn't like her. That doesn't mean I'm out there sticking it into whatever hole is going.
ROSE:	Don't use such vulgar language. There's a framed photo of John Paul II on my dresser.
GEORGE:	Fine. You want the truth? *(clearly making it up)* She was an alcoholic.
ROSE:	She never was.
GEORGE:	Pissed every night.

ROSE: Lovely girl like that. Well it does run in the family.

GEORGE: Does that satisfy you ma?

ROSE: Good job your ma is playing Cupid. Ivy Collins. Gorgeous girl. A fan of yours too. Sixteen. In her prime.

GEORGE: Behave.

ROSE: I was sixteen when I met your father.

GEORGE: I've got to focus on me fighting.

ROSE: All this fighting gets in the way of a family.

GEORGE: It's what I was born to do.

ROSE: Funny that, it's what your father died doing.

GEORGE: He'd long quit.

ROSE: Oh that tumour just turned up out of nowhere did it?

GEORGE: Given another life he'd do it again.

ROSE: He was a fool, and you're a bigger one.

GEORGE: Well get used to this idea ma. I was approached with an offer last night. From Vic Samson.

ROSE: Vic Samson! After everything your father went through.

GEORGE: I'm not my father.

ROSE:	They'll chew you up and spit you out that lot.
GEORGE:	Ma, I want more.
ROSE:	More! You're not Oliver fucking Twist. What more could you possibly want?
GEORGE:	I'll leave you to your afternoon.
ROSE:	Well I suppose I should be grateful for the five minutes of your company.
GEORGE:	Love you ma.
ROSE:	Love you too. But George…
GEORGE:	Ma?
ROSE:	Get your ass to mass.

Scene Five

Vic's gym. Dane is skipping.

DANE: Early rise. Thirty-minute jog along the canal. The morning mist slowly brings me into the day. Breakfast. Eggs. Lots of eggs. In for 8. Andy's always first.

ANDY: Ey lad, give us hand with this.

DANE: Him and me dad go way back. Andy was Vic's first trainer.

Dane helps Andy lifting some equipment.

ANDY: 'kin 'ell lad take some weight will ya? I'm on pills for me back.

DANE: Should you really be doing this?

ANDY: I'm not a cripple! We're almost there. Slides in a beauty, as my missus would say.

DANE: And one by one the gym comes to life.

Vic walks in.

DANE: Old man crawls in. Sniffs the place he's known for thirty years.

VIC: Morning.

Dane continues skipping.

VIC: Saturday. I shouldn't have walked. I'm sorry. But son, you've got to start listening to me. Believe it or not I do know what I'm talking about.

Dane continues to skip and ignore Vic.

VIC: Come on, lots to do today. I need you in the room.

Dane stops skipping.

DANE: And I need you to stay in my corner.

VIC: Like I say…

DANE: You wouldn't do that to the other lads.

VIC: The other lads wouldn't piss about son.

DANE: I won didn't I?

VIC: You've got to be putting him away inside four.

DANE: I was having a bit of fun Vic.

VIC: No fun to be had lad. You knock him out, improve your record and move on.

Dane starts skipping again.

VIC: I know you've got that Mitchell fight in your head. He survived, Dane. You hit him hard but it were a good clean hit. It happens. It's hit or be hit and, son, you cannot lose that streak.

Dane continues to skip, ignoring Vic.

VIC: Got a new lad starting today. Hoping he'll put a rocket up your arse.

DANE: Who?

VIC: He's got killer instinct. You can learn from him.

DANE: Broken fucking record.

VIC: One more thing. Paul Taylor was on the phone again this morning. Wants an interview.

DANE: He knows a good thing when he sees it. You can learn from him.

VIC: I told him no. He was talking about *rumours*.

DANE: Rumours?

VIC: Just keep that in mind lad.

Dane considers this and exits towards the changing rooms. Vic steps forward to address the lads in the gym (the audience).

VIC: Right dick heads, listen up.

Vic notices someone in the gym/audience.

Ellis, will you go easy on them protein shakes. There were a right fucking mess in bogs this morning.

Introduces an imagined George to various members of the gym/audience.

	George this is Ellis, Tyler…Logan, Kev – George. Over here this is Andy. He's like the Sammy Davis Jr. to my Sinatra. Used to be Dean Martin, then he stopped drinking.
	And somewhere over here is my son, Dane. *(Calling)* Dane get over here lad.

Vic exits. Dane appears as George enters the gym.

DANE:	Old man's voice is a woodpecker on the side of me head. White noise. Turn around, expecting some 'roid head. Instead it's this wiry little fucker with a cheeky smile.
	Who are you?
GEORGE:	George O'Connell. Call me Gorgeous George. Bare knuckle fighter, part time poet.
DANE:	*(bemused)* Right. Sorry mate, I think you've got the wrong place.
GEORGE:	The new kid in town.
DANE:	Oh yeah?
GEORGE:	Yeah. Vic tells me he needs a champion.
DANE:	Hang on Vic. This is gonna be the rocket up my arse? This pikey?
GEORGE:	Oi!
DANE:	What?

GEORGE: I'll let that go once because you're the chief's son. Call me a pikey one more time; I'll hit you so hard you'll be pissing into a bag for the rest of your life.

DANE: Fancy your chances?

GEORGE: I'll have a crack at anything me mate.

DANE: Oh yeah?

GEORGE: Yeah.

DANE: Gloves on.

Dane throws gloves to George who puts them on.

GEORGE: Love a baptism of fire.

DANE: Little fucking terrier aren't you.

GEORGE: Taken out bigger lads than you in me time.

DANE: What, bouncing off beer bellies in a car park?

GEORGE: Good scrap Saturday. Should've been there.

DANE: Sorry mate I was busy lining up a title shot.

GEORGE: Shame daddy's more interested in what I've got.

You see, poetry.

DANE: That was shit.

With both gloves on the two men step forward and touch gloves. George points his glove right up in Dane's face.

GEORGE: Guess which finger I'm sticking up.

The two back up and start to measure each other up. Dane throws two quick jabs, George slides them. They change direction, continuing to circle each other. Dane throws two rights and George sways back both times, dodging them impressively.

GEORGE: He has a swipe, he has a swing but he's never shared the ring with a Gypsy King.

Now George goes on the offensive, throwing two jabs which Dane blocks, Dane counters the second jab with a left to the body. It lands, George stumbles, Dane tries to take advantage with an overhead right, but George blocks and darts backwards to avoid further trouble. He grabs at his crotch and then swings in with a right and a left that Dane blocks and the two end up locked. Dane overpowers George and throws him back, George circles his hips, mocking Dane, before diving in again, ducking a left hook from Dane before Dane catches George unaware with a right uppercut, sending George to the canvas. Dane stands over George, replicating the famous image of Ali and Liston.

DANE: Alright mate that's enough.

GEORGE: I'm just getting started.

DANE: We're done.

GEORGE: It's gonna take more than that.

DANE: You're done.

Dane stands over George. George unstraps his gloves and offers them up to Dane who takes them off. As he does so George sticks both middle fingers up and laughs. Dane smiles. He helps George to his feet.

GEORGE: I'll let you have that one. But beware the return of the Gypsy King.

DANE: Bit fucking mad you.

GEORGE: Yeah.

DANE: If you're gonna be joining us there's something you need to know.

GEORGE: What?

DANE: Don't take locker 3. That's Psycho Pat's locker. If you take that he goes a bit…

GEORGE: Psycho?

DANE: Basically, yeah.

GEORGE: Right. Thanks.

DANE: One more thing. It's a Samson gym, 'Gorgeous' George.

Dane pats George on the cheeks as he leaves.

Scene Six

George and Rose are waiting in line for communion at mass. They speak in hushed voices.

GEORGE: It'd mean a lot to me ma.

ROSE: See her *(points)* Dives out her row every time, never lets anyone through. As though she must receive the body of our lord before us all. Selfish cow.

GEORGE: It's my first professional fight.

ROSE: Why do you put this pressure on me?

GEORGE: Bright new dawn.

ROSE: Your father's son all right.

GEORGE: I really want you there.

ROSE: Just stand here, receive the body of our lord and repent of your sins.

GEORGE: I haven't sinned.

ROSE: Jesus died for our sins.

GEORGE: Yes ma, he did.

ROSE: Jesus died for our sins and you stand before the altar proclaiming you haven't sinned.

GEORGE: Ma, we're in a church, you don't need to tell me Jesus died for our fucking sins.

ROSE: Well stop being such a cunt.

Alarmed they may have been overheard, George and Rose look around.

They then face the altar and offer the sign of the cross.

GEORGE: I haven't sinned.

ROSE: We're all sinners before our lord George O'Connell.

GEORGE: Just come to my fight will you.

ROSE: Connor's little one is being christened week after next. I want you there.

GEORGE: Of course I'll be there.

ROSE: He says you've gone quiet on him.

GEORGE: He wants me to train him.

ROSE: A good looking boy like that wanting to fight?

GEORGE: Oh thanks ma.

ROSE: With all this fighting you'll be no oil painting when you're older. Unlike your mother.

Ivy will be there. Keen to meet you. You think about that and I'll think about coming to your fight.

They both step forward.

Scene Seven

The changing rooms, Vic's gym. Late one evening after training. Dane and George are alone.

DANE: They not have showers in caravans?

GEORGE: We do. Power sockets an'all.

DANE: Nice.

GEORGE: I've got a flat me.

DANE: Fancy. You're getting better.

GEORGE: For a pikey?

DANE: Still got some way to go.

GEORGE: Do you normally swan around this place like you own it?

DANE: I kinda do 'Gorgeous' George.

GEORGE: Can you not?

DANE: Not what?

GEORGE: Call me that.

DANE: I thought *you* called you that.

GEORGE: But can you not call me that like *that*.

DANE: What's the problem with me calling you that like *that* 'Gorgeous' George?

GEORGE: Cos when you say it, it sounds a bit gay.

DANE: Well good job I am a bit gay.

GEORGE: Serious?

DANE: Very.

GEORGE: Does Vic know?

DANE: Vic and all the other lads.

GEORGE: And they don't say anything?

DANE: Well they don't exactly invite themselves round to watch. But they don't say anything, no.

GEORGE: What about your ma?

DANE: She can't say much. She's dead.

GEORGE: Fucking hell.

DANE: That's was my reaction. But when I told her she was cool.

GEORGE: So you're just…gay?

DANE: That's kinda how it works.

GEORGE: How long have you known?

DANE: Since I was a kid.

GEORGE: And no one here…

DANE: Gives a shit. Not really. Vic… well, dads are dads.

GEORGE: I lost my dad.

DANE: It's not a contest.

GEORGE: I know that dickhead. I'm saying. Your ma, my dad... I...

DANE: I get it.

GEORGE: So how did you tell your folks?

DANE: You're more interested than Paul Taylor.

GEORGE: Who?

DANE: Journo. Reckons he knows.

GEORGE: Fuck.

DANE: It won't get out.

GEORGE: How d'you know?

DANE: Vic makes sure of that.

GEORGE: Aye. He's a hard man Vic. He fought my dad. Paddy O'Connell.

DANE: O'Connell... Oh yeah, first round knockout. Bit like me and you.

GEORGE: Oh alright fuck off.

DANE: Come on, it was good.

GEORGE: Got lucky.

Dane locks his eyes on George and slowly moves towards him.

DANE: Floored by a faggot.

GEORGE: Fuck off.

DANE: Floored by a fag. Bet that was a culture shock Gorgeous George.

Dane advances on George.

DANE: I think you like it.

They cannot break each other's gaze. Dane grabs at George's crotch. George is hard.

DANE: I think you really like it.

Dane reaches inside George's pants and wanks him off until he cums. He pulls his hand out and wipes it on George.

DANE: Get a move on dick head. I've gotta lock up.

Scene Eight

The living room of Dane and Vic's house. Dane is watching TV. Josh appears.

JOSH: Surprise!

DANE: What are you doing here?

JOSH: Door was on the latch. Who are you expecting?

DANE: Josh, you can't come in.

JOSH: Frig me! You can tell a straight man rules the roost in here. That rug is vile.

DANE: My dad is gonna be back.

JOSH: And who hangs a pair of boxing gloves over a chaise longue?

DANE: Josh…

JOSH: I'm wearing those Aussiebums that you like.

DANE: My dad.

JOSH: I thought he knew.

DANE: Doesn't mean he knows about this.

JOSH: Oh what, he thinks you're a nun?

DANE: He doesn't want to see this.

JOSH: Excuse me, what's 'this'? I think it's weird you still living with him. How old are ya?

DANE: He's got no one, all right.

JOSH: But aren't you gonna want to invite me round at some point? 'Meet the in-laws'.

DANE: Not tonight Josh.

JOSH: It's normally every night with you.

DANE: Well it's not tonight.

JOSH: Fine. We'll go out. But you can lose this face.

DANE: I'm not going out.

JOSH: Oh what, stay in here and watch *(glances in the direction of where the TV would be)* politics? Or come and have some cheap drinks with me at G-A-Y.

DANE: I'm not going G-A-bleeding-Y.

JOSH: Why?

DANE: It's not for me.

JOSH: Fine. Look, the reason I come round…me mum's banging on about that meal again.

DANE: What meal?

JOSH: The one I invited you to.

DANE: Could you not have sent this over a text?

JOSH: I did.

	Anyway. Quick update. She's scrapped the Dauphinoise and we're having a gratin.
DANE:	No.
JOSH:	Oh a few carbs won't kill.
DANE:	It's not that...
JOSH:	Fine. I'll ask her to do some sweet potatoes and curly kale.
DANE:	I don't want to meet them.

Beat.

JOSH:	Ever?
DANE:	No.
JOSH:	Oh. So that's it then?
DANE:	Yeah. I'm sorry.
JOSH:	So what was I? Just somewhere to park your bike?
DANE:	Don't talk like that.
JOSH:	A bay to drop your anchor...
DANE:	Do you have to...
JOSH:	...a port in a storm...
DANE:	...stop it...
JOSH:	...or was I just a fuck?

DANE: You know what, yeah you were.

JOSH: And the truth will out.

DANE: I've told you, I'm sorry.

JOSH: I don't need pity Dane. I'm fine. I've got Tinder for the nice boys, Scruff for the dirty boys and Grindr for the *closet* cases.

The sound of the front door opening.

DANE: That's me dad. Can you stop with the drama?

JOSH: Oh there's gonna be drama.

Josh struts out of the room in the direction of the oncoming Vic.

Scene Nine

The next morning. Vic is addressing the gym/audience.

VIC: Right dick heads, listen up. Gonna move things around a bit in here. Change is as good as a rest etc. etc. Me and George have really gotta step things up now. Showtime's approaching. Changes won't affect most of you but Dane, you'll be working with Andy for a bit. He'll see you right.

DANE: It's not happening.

VIC: It is happening and it's for the best.

DANE: Everyone knows I'm king of this castle.

VIC: Well you've just lost your head, y'majesty.

DANE: I'm the reason people still know about you.

VIC: Without my surname you'd be nothing. *(Turns to a member of the audience)* Right Ellis, I'm gonna say this slow because you lad are thick…

DANE: Oh I get it. This isn't about boxing. This is about last night.

VIC: That'll do…

DANE: Scared word will get out? Paul Taylor might be onto something…

VIC: He's onto nothing…

DANE:	Might find out your only son…
VIC:	*(erupts)* That is enough!
	You disappeared up your own arse a long time ago. I've been soft for not stamping it. Get out lad.
DANE:	Fine. I will.
VIC:	Well go on then.
DANE:	I'll give Flannigans a call.
VIC:	Flannigans!
DANE:	Gary's been after me for years.
VIC:	Last time they produced a champion you weren't even an itch in my pants.
DANE:	Reckon they could have one soon.

Dane storms out of the gym.

Scene Ten

George's flat. Later that night. George is preparing a sofa bed.

GEORGE: One night.

DANE: I'm on the sofa bed?

GEORGE: I like my space. So he's kicked you out?

DANE: It's not the fifties, I left. Not a bad place this.

GEORGE: Better than a caravan.

DANE: Got enough photos haven't you?

GEORGE: Big family.

DANE: My place it's just pictures of me dad.

GEORGE: This is the only place you could think of?

DANE: One of them, yeah.

Dane shoots a cheeky smile at George.

GEORGE: What was it about, this row?

DANE: He come home early last night, I was with this guy.

GEORGE: Oh.

DANE: Not like that.

GEORGE: So is this guy your boyfriend or…

DANE: No he's just a fu… just a guy.

GEORGE: So why aren't you with this guy now?

DANE: Not getting jealous are you 'Gorgeous' George? Don't worry. You're hotter.

George likes this. He turns to face Dane. They stare at each other for a moment. George and Dane kiss. George reaches into Dane's pants. Dane backs off.

DANE: What you doing?

GEORGE: What you want.

DANE: What?

George reaches into Dane's pants again.

DANE: No, George.

GEORGE: But that's why you're here.

DANE: No its not.

GEORGE: What about the changing rooms?

DANE: I don't wanna wank you off every time I see you.

GEORGE: But I thought you were gay.

Dane starts to laugh.

GEORGE: Stop laughing Dane. Stop laughing at me. Stop it!

Dane stops laugh. George looks uneasy.

DANE: Are you okay?

GEORGE: You're messing with me head now. I don't know what this is. You come round – you're here – but I don't know what you want.

Dane kisses George.

DANE: That.

GEORGE: Just that?

DANE: Yeah. Sometimes it can just be a hug.

Dane hugs George.

GEORGE: Like this?

DANE: Yeah.

GEORGE: This how you normally do it?

DANE: From what I remember.

Dane holds George tighter. George hugs him back, smiling.

GEORGE: So this is alright?

DANE: Yeah.

Dane brings George over to the bed and holds him in his arms.

GEORGE: What else can we do?

DANE: Could go on a date.

GEORGE: A date?

DANE: You ever been on one?

GEORGE: I'm very in demand.

DANE:	I'm sure you are. So where did you take the last date?
GEORGE:	Took her round the back of Asda car park.
DANE:	Nice.
GEORGE:	It really wasn't.
DANE:	Sunday?
GEORGE:	Where?
DANE:	You decide. Just not Asda car park.

Scene Eleven

A screen in a cinema. George and Dane take their seats.

DANE: Is this what you call a date? Cinema in the middle of nowhere.

GEORGE: Cinema was your idea.

DANE: Only because you suggested KFC.

What's wrong with the place round the corner from yours?

GEORGE: Don't be stupid.

DANE: Because two blokes don't go see a movie?

GEORGE: Not at eleven in the morning they don't.

DANE: And for good reason. Its kid's films.

GEORGE: It's meant to be alright this. At least it's just us.

George looks around the cinema. Realising no one else is there, he kisses Dane.

DANE: So how does this compare with Asda car park?

GEORGE: Kicking its ass. Look.

George pulls out a packet of Pom-Bear crisps and Haribo sweets.

GEORGE: *(pointing in the general direction of the cinema staff)* And not one of them bastards caught me.

DANE: They're on minimum wage, I'm not sure they care.

GEORGE: Want one?

DANE: No.

GEORGE: Good cos you're not having one.

DANE: What are they?

GEORGE: Pom-Bears.

DANE: Ey?

GEORGE: Gotta love a Pom-Bear. 5 packs for a 50p down the Home Bargains.

DANE: And your first fight is when?

GEORGE: Yeah but they're only Pom-Bears. Go on, I'll let you have one.

DANE: I'm not having a fucking Pom-Bear.

GEORGE: You're not in training.

DANE: Not at that gym I'm not.

GEORGE: So live life and have a Pom-Bear.

DANE: I've told you. I'm done with him.

GEORGE: He's good to me Vic.

DANE: You should tell him we're fucking and see how good he is then.

GEORGE: You said he were alright really.

DANE: He is. If you stay out of sight.

GEORGE: My dad caught me in ma's clothes once.

DANE: *(sniggering)* No?

GEORGE: Yeah. We used to have this little dwarf aunty called Edna. She used to host tea parties. Now this one time she couldn't make it. So I went as Edna.

DANE: That's well funny.

GEORGE: Dad comes home early. There's me in me ma's dressing gown and bra dancing to 'Brown Girl In The Ring'.

Dane pisses himself laughing. George joins in. They have a moment.

DANE: What did he say?

GEORGE: "I want a Gypsy King", he says. "Don't want a Gypsy Queen".

Next day he takes me down his gym. Made me stand there with me hands by me side, while he got some practice in.

George punches the open palm of his hand.

My nose squelched as it broke. Like walking in wet shoes. He had me in that gym every day from then on.

DANE: Call it a draw.

GEORGE: You'd miss him though.

George kisses Dane. George then slides down to his knees.

DANE: What are you doing? We're in a cinema!

GEORGE: It's dead in here. Like being at one of your fights.

DANE: Prick! Go on then, quick.

George starts giving Dane head. The sound of the door to the cinema screen opening and a group of toddlers is heard. Dane pushes George down onto the floor.

DANE: George pack it in.

GEORGE: Why?

DANE: There's a load of mums and kids.

GEORGE: Shit!

DANE: Ssssh!

(Turns attention to the mums and toddler group) Morning.

George goes to get up. Dane holds him down.

DANE: You're gonna have to stay there for the film.

GEORGE: How long is this film?

DANE: An hour, maybe two.

GEORGE: Stinks down here.

DANE: *(To the group in front)* Yeah, I love a Disney me.

GEORGE: She's gonna think you're a right weirdo. Sat on the back row like Jimmy Savile.

DANE: Ssssh.

Another moment passes and then George's phone goes off. He scrambles to get it out his pocket and drops it.

DANE: Fuck's sake! *(realising the parents have overheard this)* I am so sorry!

Dane goes down to meet George.

DANE: Answer it.

GEORGE: I've dropped it.

DANE: Where?

GEORGE: Ooh, ooh…

DANE: You got it?

GEORGE: No, but I found a quid.

DANE: Here it is.

Dane passes George his phone and he answers.

GEORGE: Ma…no, no I haven't forgotten…sorry ma you're breaking up.

Hangs up.

GEORGE: I'm meant to be at a christening.

DANE: What should we do?

GEORGE: Grab me Pom-Bears.

They slowly stand. It is clear the parents of the toddlers have seen them both.

GEORGE: Leg it!

They run out of the cinema.

Scene Twelve

George runs into the christening. Rose stands waiting for him with a bottle of beer in hand.

ROSE: You'd be late to your own funeral.

GEORGE: Sorry ma, I had stuff to do.

ROSE: Stuff to do! Here, you need to catch up.

She offers George a drink. He takes a swig, then spits it out, coughing loudly and pulling a face.

GEORGE: What's in that?

ROSE: Pepper. Teach you to be late.

GEORGE: Jesus Christ!

ROSE: Don't blaspheme you little cunt. Come here. There's someone I want you to meet.

GEORGE: I'm not in the mood.

ROSE: *(calling)* Ivy, get over here flower.

GEORGE: No ma, I'm really not in the mood.

ROSE: Lovely girl. Not like most of your harlots.

GEORGE: What, her with two pints and a septic nose piercing?

ROSE: Ivy! Well look at you. Sure, on the seventh day the lord didn't rest, he was too busy making you bloody perfect. Ivy, this is my son George. I'll leave you two lovebirds to it.

GEORGE: Wait, ma, you can't leave me here…

After a moment, Ivy enters.

IVY: Alright? Our Jackie's got a spare snakebite if you want it.

GEORGE: I'm good.

IVY: Bet you are. I like a fighter me.

GEORGE: Imagine you can handle yourself.

IVY: Rose said you've gone all pro. I could go a few rounds with you. But I'm saving myself.

GEORGE: Is your nose ok?

IVY: Aaah ey, is it oozing again?

GEORGE: Go and get that sorted.

IVY: Look at you dishing out your orders. Hope you're gonna be like that on our wedding night.

GEORGE: Wedding night?

IVY: Yeah! You're gonna have to wait til then, I'm no slag.

GEORGE: Who said anything about a wedding night?

IVY: Rose.

GEORGE: She said that?

IVY: Me ma's been looking at venues.

GEORGE: Look sweetheart you've got it wrong.

IVY: And you wanna see the dress George. It's got sequins, angel wings and a big fuck off train longer than the Mersey.

GEORGE: Sounds delightful. But we're not getting married.

IVY: But Rose said!

GEORGE: Well Rose is a mad old bitch who shouldn't have said.

IVY: You're a wrongun George O'Connell.

GEORGE: There's nowt wrong with me.

IVY: Go fuck yourself with a tent pole! Ma!

Ivy exits. George stands in exasperation. He turns, notices someone in the pub (audience).

GEORGE: *(calling)* Little Bill! Bill?

No response. George turns around as Connor enters.

CONNOR: Georgey boy. The lads said you'd shown up.

GEORGE: Well they didn't let on.

CONNOR: Can I have a word?

GEORGE: Let me guess. You wanna cancel tomorrow's session?

CONNOR: To be honest I'm not sure I want to be trained by you anymore.

GEORGE:	I knew it. No stomach.
CONNOR:	I'm not sure I wanna be taught what you're learning.
GEORGE:	How do you mean?
CONNOR:	What you've been learning at that gym. With that dirty boy?
GEORGE:	What dirty boy?
CONNOR:	Vic's son. Hear you and him make good sparring partners.
GEORGE:	Something you wanna say Connor?
CONNOR:	Why has he been round your flat all week?

This hits George.

	Bobby Roy saw you. I told you George, I don't like you being out of sight.
GEORGE:	Connor…
CONNOR:	Just imagine what would happen if I told every O'Connell in here.
GEORGE:	We're family.
CONNOR:	Then be an O'Connell. These country folk have got to you. Think of yer ma. So proud of her 'Gorgeous' George. Bring him back. Bring back the Gypsy King.

Scene Thirteen

A ward in a hospital. Josh lies in bed with a patch over one eye. Dane approaches.

DANE: Josh.

JOSH: What are you doing here?

DANE: Your mam said I could have a minute.

JOSH: You actually spoke to her.

DANE: How you feeling?

JOSH: Well I'm on more pills than Liza but I'll survive.

DANE: What happened?

JOSH: After you fucked me off I got on the grind, didn't I. Got invited to an orgy. I was the centerpiece. Should've seen the lad who got me round, gorgeous he was. He was like Colin Farrell, and you know I like me Irish. Arms out here. Built like a brick shit house. And the others. Scallies. Skin heads. It was a council estate porno.

DANE: What did they do?

Beat.

DANE: Come on Josh tell me.

JOSH: Well first they made me lie in a bathtub and drink their piss. Never been into watersports.

	Then, like I say, I was the centerpiece. They grabbed a bat and took it in turns.
DANE:	Shit.
JOSH:	Think they've knocked the sight out of this eye. Other one's fine though. And hey, I'm bringing eye patches back in. I'm a skinny, white Gabrielle.
DANE:	Did you say they were on Grindr?
JOSH:	Yeah.
DANE:	Is their profile still up?
JOSH:	I don't know Dane.
DANE:	Hang on, do you remember where they lived?
JOSH:	Dane…
DANE:	Because I'll go round…
JOSH:	You'll go nowhere. You are not my boyfriend! You're just a *fuck*. Remember?

This hurts Dane and Josh can see it. He softens.

	Ey, your training wasn't wasted. Hooked one of them with a jab.
DANE:	*(smiling)* You can't hook a jab.
JOSH:	Y'what?
DANE:	You hook or you jab.

JOSH: Oh.

They both chuckle.

DANE: I'm sorry, yeah?

JOSH: Frigging hell. Wizard of Oz gave the Tin Man a heart. But you're more the cowardly lion aren't you? No courage. Oh come on Dane, we're all friends of Dorothy's.

DANE: Stop with the stupid comments.

JOSH: What? Too gay?

DANE: Look at you.

JOSH: You can. With two eyes. But I may never see out of this eye again so I'll say whatever I want. The whole time I was there, I was harder than you. Because I was honest about who I am. I think I'm rather fabulous and I'm never going to hide that. I just wish you'd realise what might happen if you could do the same.

DANE: It's not that easy.

JOSH: I know. But look at me. I'm still here. Sat like Pudsey fucking bear. But I'm still here.

Scene Fourteen

Dane and George sit on separate sides of the stage, facing out, giving their respective interviews to local journalist Paul Taylor (not present).

DANE: You got your interview Paul, I hope you're ready... I don't see it as brave, coming out... My mum didn't give a shit. She'd have squared up to anyone who did. And she had a better left hook than my dad...

GEORGE: Taylor... me and the lads read your interview with Dane. Now there's something I wanna say...

George composes himself.

Vic were right to kick him out. So what if it's his son? That's why Vic's a winner, yeah. He's ruthless.

DANE: I'm not making any comment on my dad...

GEORGE: The other lads don't want that in the changing rooms...

DANE: For a long time, I asked myself the same question. How can a fighter be gay? But I'm the same boxer I've always been. Better even...

GEORGE: Boxing is a traditional sport. Like me. Traditional. That's how I were raised... I learned you can't go far wrong with the word of the lord by your side...

DANE: I thought about quitting, walking away. But there could be boxing fans out there going through what I've been through. To them I'd say…

GEORGE: "If a man lieth with mankind as he lieth with a woman he has committed an abomination".

DANE: I'd say…

GEORGE: Unequivocal. That is the word of God.

DANE: Be who you are. Feels like things are changing. Look at me getting all Nelson Mandela. Fucking hell.

GEORGE: And they can get married now can't they? What next? Marrying your dog, your daughter, it's just wrong.

DANE: Am I seeing someone at the moment?

GEORGE: The devil thrives on debauchery, we have to be strong.

DANE: No.

Scene Fifteen

Vic's gym. Andy and Vic moving equipment.

VIC: Every bleeding paper.

ANDY: Vic.

VIC: Front page in some.

ANDY: Give us hand with this.

VIC: What about them lot camped outside the gym this morning?

ANDY: Parasites.

VIC: They'll be here all week.

ANDY: Vic, would you give me a hand with this?

Vic moves over and starts helping Andy.

ANDY: Now, you want my advice?

VIC: No, but I've a feeling I'm gonna get it.

ANDY: You get rid of George. They'll soon disappear.

VIC: And who does that leave us with? Ellis flaming 'Bomber' Brown?

ANDY: He's not right for us Vic. It's about the reputation of this gym.

VIC: Drop it.

ANDY: Talk to Dane.

VIC: I'm warning you, drop it.

ANDY: I'll drop you in a minute!

VIC: I was trying to protect him. You know as well as I do, this world – the boxing world – it ain't ready for… that.

ANDY: He's lost his mam, Vic. He needs his dad.

VIC: That's a low blow Andy.

ANDY: Maybe. But I were with you in that hospital. You promised her you'd look after him.

Vic stares at Andy. A moment passes.

VIC: I'm going the arena.

Storms off.

ANDY: Wait, Vic!

Andy follows Vic.

Scene Sixteen

The stage is split again between two worlds, reminiscent of the opening scene.

DANE: A week in the spotlight. Photos, flashes, smiles and winks. New doors have opened and I've been welcomed in. A hero, they say.

But what's a hero that doesn't fight? Ain't been near that gym for weeks. Any gym for weeks. And I know I shouldn't care and I shouldn't be aware...

But tonight's his fight. I've read and heard the words he said but I can't help myself. I climb the arena steps to see him once again.

George enters into this spotlight, other side of the stage.

GEORGE: The Gypsy King is back in the ring!

An ugly wee fucker moves in and out, all the time trying, testing my chin. He lands consistent, but with little power, and a jaw more iron by the hour I'm rocking it one round in.

Bell. Corner. Vic stood silent offers nothing still.

To hell with it.

DANE: And there, in his corner, Vic. Two traitors side by side. Father and son.

	The two can rot together. This was a stupid idea. I'm calling it here.
GEORGE:	Round three. Crowd loving me. But there's someone else I start to see.
	It's Dane who's ringside in my head. And I don't feel so gorgeous now. All of this means nothing if I can't have him.
	BANG!
	Blindsided. Uppercut. Shit.
DANE:	The arena just behind me I pick up the pace.
	"Gorgeous George, na na na, Gorgeous George na na na."
	I carry on with rage inside at the mention of his name.
	I pass a pub, a group of lads too pissed to stand. Fingers pointing, smirking. A shout is sent my way.
	Head down, straight on. Shortcut through an alleyway.
	A noise behind. I've been followed.
	"Oi faggot!"
GEORGE:	BANG!
	My legs feel weak, the ropes seem safe. Right now I'm hanging in.

DANE: "That pikey in the paper were right about you."

Once more. Head down, straight on.

GEORGE: I hold him off. A counter punch. I smile through blood. I line one up.

Vic throws in the towel.

And then the towel flies in.

Vic?

The ref waves his arms, the fans react, this fight is through.

George turns to Vic.

It's a drop of blood, a papercut, why have you thrown it in?

VIC: You've made your choice son. Now I've made mine.

GEORGE: He's gone. He's done. I've lost and he's…

George shakes his head and sits back in his corner.

DANE: He's back. Blocks my way. Spitting words, homophobic rage.

And then I see the blade.

A swipe, a swish, a sidestep takes me out of reach. His guard is down.

BANG. He drops. I follow him with two rights, a left and then I picture George and I know I can't stop.

With every hit his blood pours thick.

And then his eyes meet mine. He's just a boy. Nothing more to say.

I see his life slip away.

Scene Seventeen

The changing rooms after George's fight. George is taking off his gloves. We hear Rose approaching.

ROSE: Who do you think you're talking to young man? I'll go where I damn well please. I'm his mother. Where do you think he got the name 'Gorgeous' from?

Rose enters the changing rooms.

GEORGE: What are you doing here?

ROSE: I gave you my word. I can't say I enjoyed it but your heads still on its shoulders so I'll thank the lord for that.

GEORGE: Thank the lord for nothing ma. I lost.

ROSE: I've given you worse clips round the ear when you were a lad, I can tell you.

GEORGE: I know that. Vic screwed me. Threw the towel in. I were fine.

ROSE: I warned you. You stray from your own kind and this is what happens. I could see the ghost of your father rising above you.

GEORGE: Ma, this is nothing to do with me father. It's about me. What I did.

Rose pulls out a newspaper. It contains George's interview.

ROSE: This? It's a terrible photograph, but an interesting read…

> "If a man lieth with a man he has committed an abomination…and shall surely be put to death."

From the boxing ring to the pulpit.

GEORGE: I didn't mean it.

ROSE: Then why say it?

GEORGE: I were scared.

ROSE: Scared? These are strong words indeed. If I was Vic I'd have done worse than throw in the towel. Talking about his boy like that.

GEORGE: I did it for the family.

ROSE: The family?

I took this interview of yours to Father Howard. He's a nice man. Awful coffee breath but a nice man. I suppose he's what you'd call one of these modern priests. He would seem to disagree with you. If that's truly what you think.

But I don't think it is, is it? So come on, out with it.

George is speechless.

ROSE: Oh for goodness sake George O'Connell this is like pulling teeth! I don't think you'll ever bring home a girl, will you?

George slowly shakes his head.

ROSE: And you couldn't tell me. Did I not raise you to be honest? Your father was a crook but he had his principles. Number one, honesty.

GEORGE: You knew?

ROSE: Of course I knew. I'm your mother. And I remember Aunt Edna's tea parties.

George laughs. He is stunned by his ma's understanding reaction.

GEORGE: All those women?

ROSE: Those streetwalkers? It was a test.

GEORGE: Why?

ROSE: I needed to hear it from you. And yer man?

George points to the newspaper.

ROSE: You don't need to be Miss fucking Marple to work that one out.

GEORGE: I really messed up.

ROSE: A bit of time heals all wounds.

Rose can see he is struggling and instinctively mothers him. She pulls out a thermos flask.

ROSE: Time… and Bovril. Loved his Bovril. A chunky wee toddler you were, other kids with bottles of milk and you with a big old bottle of Bovril.

George smiles and takes it.

ROSE: Won't you say grace?

GEORGE: For what we are about to receive...

The sound of George's phone receiving a text message. George checks it.

ROSE: Phones off during grace.

GEORGE: It's him.

ROSE: Yer man?

GEORGE: Wants me to meet him at the gym.

ROSE: Well don't just sit there like a cunt. Go on with you George. Be happy.

GEORGE: Thanks ma.

George kisses Rose on the cheek, hands her the flask of Bovril and leaves. Rose goes to sip some Bovril, stopping as she realises she hasn't said grace.

ROSE: For what we are about to receive may the lord make us truly grateful.

Scene Eighteen

The gym, later that night. Dane his stood in a bloodied top. George enters.

GEORGE: Dane! Dane?

George moves closer towards him and reaches out for him. Dane turns. George can see the blood on his top and his hands.

DANE: Ninth fight I had. Mike Mitchell. Young lad, nothing of him. My dad wants me to hit him harder and harder. He were in a coma for three days. Promised I'd never fight like that again.

GEORGE: And have you?

DANE: Guy came at me with a blade. He called me an abomination. An abomination.

GEORGE: I'm really, really sorry.

DANE: Shame my dad was at the wrong fight. He'd have been proud of me.

GEORGE: You don't know what happened tonight do ya? Your dad threw the towel in on me.

Dane looks at George confused.

GEORGE: He did. I was fine. And he did it for you. So I reckon he is proud of you, yeah. Dane, I know I messed up but I'm gonna put it right.

DANE: Killer instinct. Found it, didn't I.

The realisation slowly dawns on George.

GEORGE: You don't mean he's...

Dane nods. George has a moment to process this. Then he realises...

GEORGE: Wait. If he come at you with a blade it were self defence.

DANE: This wasn't self defence.

GEORGE: We'll go police. They'll agree.

DANE: They're on their way.

GEORGE: They're coming here?

DANE: That's why I called you. Wanted to see this place one last time. Wanted to see you one last time. Now go.

GEORGE: I'm going nowhere.

DANE: Go.

GEORGE: Not happening.

DANE: George.

GEORGE: I want this.

DANE: No.

GEORGE: I want us. I get it now, Dane. I get it. I know what this is. Sometimes it's a kiss and sometimes it's a hug. And now I get it, I can't leave. You can't leave me.

75

DANE: I'm scared.

GEORGE: Me too.

You know what I do when I'm scared?

We hear sirens. George looks frantically around the room and picks up a pair of boxing gloves and pads from the trays under the bench, offering the gloves to Dane.

GEORGE: Put them on.

DANE: What you doing?

GEORGE: Nothing better than twatting a pad as hard as you can.

DANE: Especially if you're holding it.

GEORGE: That's it! You won't get me this time.

Dane starts putting his gloves on, buying into this.

DANE: Fancy your chances?

GEORGE: I'm serious. I'm going nowhere.

DANE: Can't get rid of you, can I?

GEORGE: No. I'm like herpes.

DANE: You may have lost, but you looked hot.

GEORGE: How would you know?

DANE: I was there. For the first round. Wouldn't have missed it for the world.

George laughs to hide back tears.

GEORGE: I might be hot. But you're gorgeous.

Sirens get louder. Dane gets distracted, George bangs the pads together.

GEORGE: Come on Dane!

DANE: Hope you're ready.

The flashing of police lights as Dane throws a combination, then another and then another before collapsing into George's arms.

Lights fade.

The End.